Mel Bay's MORE FUN W....

TRUMPET

Big Note — Easy Solos

BY WILLIAM BAY

More fun with the Trumpet is a collection of well-known, favorite melodies arranged in solo form for the beginning student. The Trumpet, Clarinet, Flute, and Trombone texts may be played together in ensemble if so desired. All the music contained in this book was designed to provide the beginning student with a wealth of musical fun and satisfaction. We hope this text will give the student hours of musical enjoyment.

TABLE OF CONTENTS

Bb TRUMPET FINGERING CHART

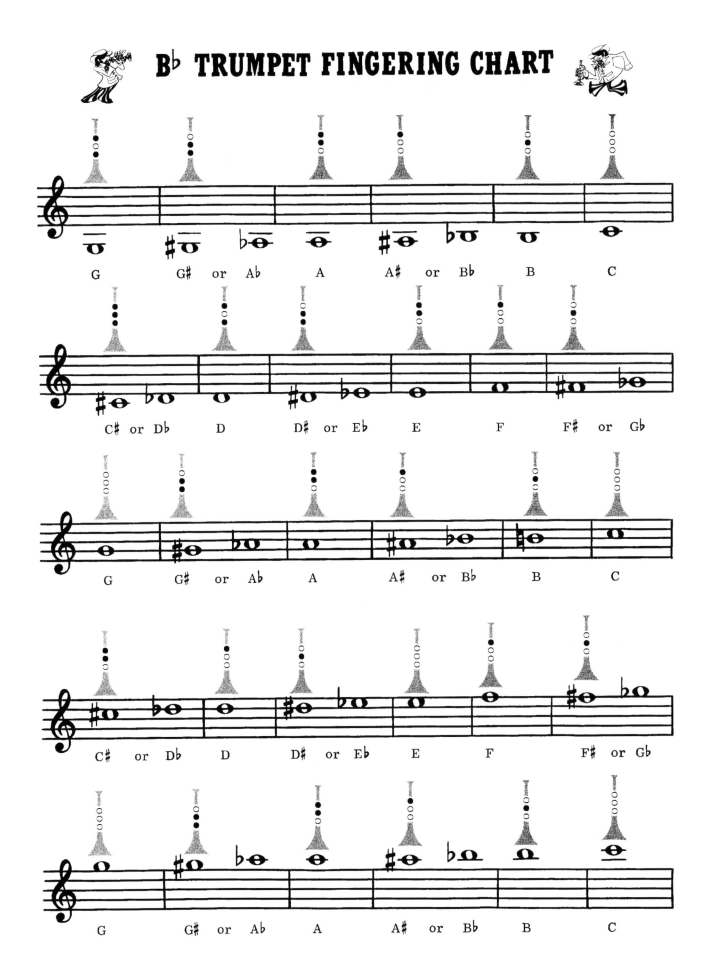

Wade in the Water

Medium Swing Tempo

Spiritual

How Firm A Foundation

Early American Hymn

My Bonnie Dearie

Scottish Folk Song

Wondrous Love

Early American Hymn

Amazing Grace

Early American Hymn

The Gal I Left Behind Me

Brisk Tempo

Song of the West

O My Darling Clementine

Simple Gifts

Shaker Song

Moderatly

America

Boldly

Ol' Dan Tucker

Fast Tempo

Folk Song

Haul Away Joe

Moderately

Sea Song

The Marines' Hymn

The Caissons

10

One More Day

Slowly

Sea Chantey

Shady Grove

Fast Tempo

Old Southern Banjo Song

Variation

11

Walls of Jericho

Swing Tempo

Spiritual

All Through The Night

Slowly

Welsh Song

Moderately

Blow Ye Winds

Song of the Sea

America, The Beautiful

Katharine Bates

Samuel A. Ward

Peacherine Rag

Scott Joplin

Medium Swing Tempo

Sailor's Hornpipe

Medium Tempo

Fiddle Tune

14

Come And Go With Me

Spiritual

Lively Tempo

The Midnight Special

Swing Tempo

Folk Song

15

I Know Where I'm Goin'

Scottish Hymn

Praise To The Lord

Favorite Hymn

At A Georgia Camp Meeting

Old Banjo Song

Lively Tempo

Henry Martin

Sunny's Blues

Blues Song

Buffalo Gals

Western Song

Old Joe Clark

Old Banjo Tune

Sailing, Sailing

Sea Song

Cielito Lindo

Mexican Song

The Easy Winners

Scott Joplin

Medium RAG Tempo

Appalachain Melody

Bright Tempo

Folk Song

Chester

Song of the Revolutionary War

Lively Tempo

Gary Owen

Bagpipe Song

Lively Tempo

Soldiers Joy

Lively Tempo

Old Fiddle Tune

Go Tell It On The Mountain

Slowly

Spiritual

rit.

All My Trials

Medium Tempo

Spiritual

O Come, O Come, Emmanuel

Slow, Flowing Tempo

12th Century

Coventry Carol

Slowly

Old English

The Ship That Never Returned

Sea Song

Peppy Tempo

Minor Melody

Hymn

Slowly

28

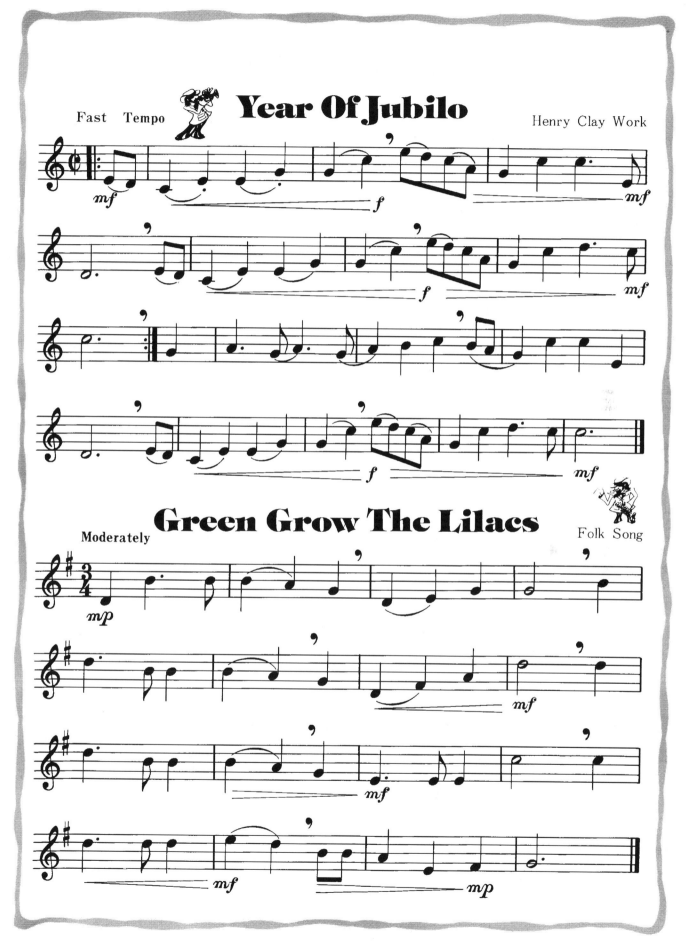

Swanee River

Stephen Foster

My Old Kentucky Home

Stephen Foster

Tenting Tonight

Slowly

Civil War Song

Angels We Have Heard On High

French Carol

Moderately

31

Ragtime Dance

Scott Joplin

Cumberland Gap

Banjo Tune

Made in the USA
Middletown, DE
15 October 2017